Ashpoems

© George Vassilacopoulos, 2025

This book is copyright. Aside from fair dealing for the purposes of study, research, criticism, review or as otherwise permitted under the Copyright Act 1968, no part may be reproduced by any process without written permission from the author.

National Library of Australia
Cataloguing – in – Publication entry:
Vassilacopoulos, George, author.
Title: Ashpoems

Cover image: Kosta Vassilacopoulos
Page layout: Frixos Ioannides

Published by re.press

ISBN: 978-0-6487282-9-0

Ashpoems

George Vassilacopoulos

MELBOURNE 2025

Acknowledgements

Many thanks to Paul Ashton, Frixos Ioannides, Elias Diacolabrianos, Toula Nicolacopoulos and Kosta Vassilacopoulos for their assistance with this publication and comments on the poems.

to Toula and Kosta

You come to me
A couple of breaths away
I can hear them
In my mouth
Gasping your arrival
'You exorcize God
With the smell of love' you say
Filling me with your whispering
Emptying me into galaxies
Of floating glories

We are still far
From the stone the poet brought us
To measure the earth
Rolling it

How can I recite you
A poem
Made from ashes?
I wrote it with my finger
Surfing on their soft silence
They fell from the sky
Perhaps it was the afternoon light burning
Or human skin and bones
How can the poet tell?
I curved my palm to give a place
To their dark tiny crystals
Words magically appeared
Little ashmemories

You are
The morning secret
My night failed to decipher
Is it too late for another night?
Too late for the late comer that I am?
I will bring you ashmemories
And the fear that harnessed my name
From your lips

Give me back to my name
So it no longer feels an orphan of sounds
Then say it again
With the ancient voice
Waiting to be whispered
In the crevices of their silence

In the morning
Unborn children
Greet us
With the patience of the poem

I circle around you into the night
Through the little voids
In my voice
Filling the room
Carried to you by their oblivion

Every me in me has a place there
A place
Where breathing stops
And the dreams of mind
Are of the same colour

Feel my body
With their memory

Whisper me into oblivion
By reciting this poem
Written voids ago
Somewhere nowhere

Awakened
The world in me
Reveals the secret of killers
Each word carries
With the lightness of the air

Together we breath in the ancient vowels of our tribe

In the morning coffee
I hear demons whispering the rhythm of my day
Words for ever angry at the sorrow of centuries
The calmness of the sofa does not mind me
It shares its shape and lets me be

As you speak orphan words
You move the void with your hands
Silently giving it the shape of their sound
You
Sound of what never became

I watch
Listening
To my poem retreating
In your breath

Half-dream
I am in you reciting ashwords
My poems hold your voice in the air
Wings of angels
I stole them one night
Abandoned
They were praying
To their palms

In this forest of long shadows
Forgotten by God
Forgotten by people
People dance the vision
Dark columns full of earth and sea and air
And fire
At the beginning there was their welcoming

Each time
I no longer claim you
You speak monsters to me
They dance around
As if I were not there
I become their secret
'This world is the whispering of demons', you say
Listening to your words with my poem

One day healers will arrive
Carrying our ancient knowledge
On wounds of innocence

I am the yesterday
Of this spring day that has forgotten
The orphans who gave birth to this world
I can teach you fear
With my ashpoems
Drops of void
Hanging
From your lips

You
Taste their heaviness
And listen
Who arrives first

You keep coming back to the warmth
Of my darkness
To my words of consonants
They tell the story of the world again
This time beginning with the camel in the desert
Studying the winds in her footprints

With my mouth hailing
The void
I fathom your eternity

I am the nobody of the vision
Full of centuries
Loving you
Like nobody
Become the note
Of this melody
Coming from the future
To us strangers to life
We grow old into the words we speak
Dancing each other
Into oblivion

Between my ashwords
As your witness
You traverse their little silences
Then wait and wait
For their solitude
To gather me
Into your story

I hang letters from my fingers
To decipher the whisper in your lips
Reciting me
With their sound

In the mornings of sorrows
Over a cup of coffee
I sing you the prayer of the poem
Can you hear the words
Limping in my lips
Carrying the heaviness of worlds
From one to the other?

I breath you in
I breath me out

Sighs of stillness floating
Around your forehead
This aura
Of frozen memories

I am me
Stuttering
The elsewhere in you

It arrives uninvited
No poet knows when
Or how
It lands in the crevice
Of my lips
And darkens my voice

I am the last prayer
Of the forgotten tribe

I bring words
For you to shatter into oblivion
With the weight of your breath
We no longer need the centuries of lies

The sound of dispersed letters
Floating in our lips
Little prophets
Consonants that promise
To speak to us vowels
Of wonder

'We are drops of the world
Sweating' you whispered
Flooding my mouth with your breath

I listened
Mouthing my solitude

The poem
Silences my words
Into little caves

Recite me
And listen to the ancient echo
Of your breathing

Pulsating into each other
From one word to the next
We become night rhythms
Carrying
The dead of the tribe
Into aethereal heights

We float
In the vertigo
Hollowed by the poets

Between worlds
The poem suspends us
Into our greyed solitude

We are prophesies of the abyss
Whispering

My words roll
Creases of history
You wait for them
Open mouth in the void
As they land
They recite us
Into stalactites

With nights for wings
You fly into darkness
Blessing my words
With the patience of the dead
To believe in resurrections

Stutter my rubble
And give me a name

Our hands weave our bodies
With the void
Into cloaks of night rhythms

We sway
In each other's breathing
Fathoming their silence

You stutter
Sighs of broken words
Out of this world

Between
Breathing in and out
You
Moment of eternity

I springle your abyss
With poems
Redeeming us with surprises

I gather
The elsewhere in you
Around my neck
Into a charm
For the bad omens
Of the next poem

Nobody
Recites our bodies
Ruined temples
Of tomorrow

You
Voiding words
In my mouth
My echo
Approaches from the distant

Hanging from your lips
I become the bell
Of all sounds

You float
Into the half dream
Of my poem
The other half
Walls
That keep the wind out

Breath its silence
And
Spit the echo of the void
Into words

Return our tribe
To the beginning

I sprinkle history
With vowels and consonants
Not to forget me

With the ancient silence of my hands
I wash your face

Begin again
To resist beginning
You are the blessed one

I wave
Retracting words
In my mouth
From the first and last
Poem
One by one

Baptized
In the mist
Of your silence
I am ready to be named
By you
Holding the empty mirror

Ashes to ashes

www.ingramcontent.com/pod-product-compliance
Lightning Source LLC
Chambersburg PA
CBHW032135090426
42743CB00007B/605